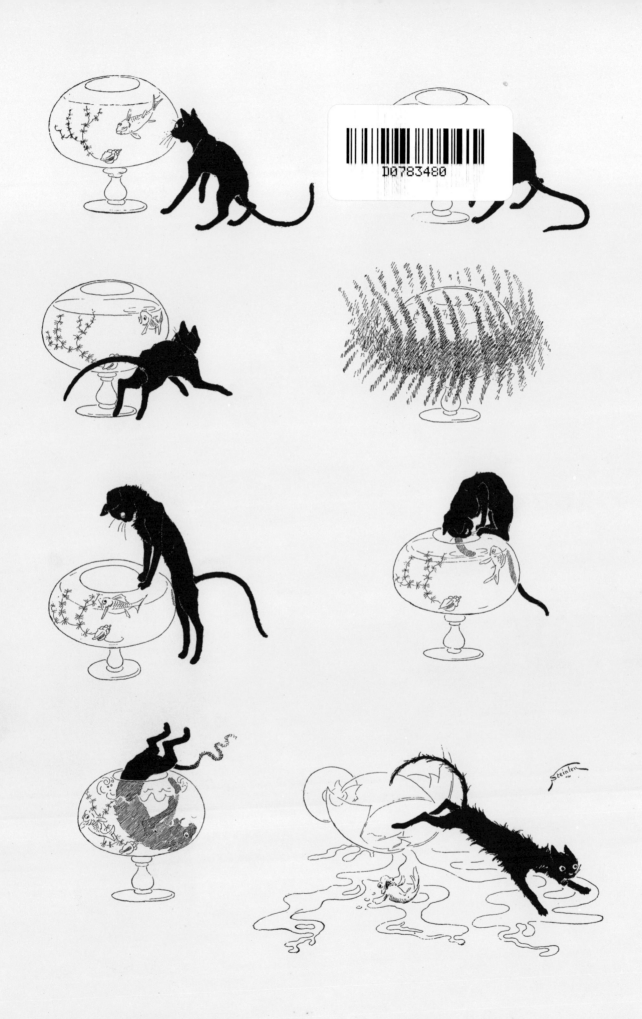

The Rum Tum Tugger is a Curious Cat:
If you offer him pheasant he would rather have grouse.
If you put him in a house he would much prefer a flat,
If you put him in a flat then he'd rather have a house.
If you set him on a mouse then he only wants a rat,
If you set him on a rat then he'd rather chase a mouse.
Yes the Rum Tum Tugger is a Curious Cat—
    And there isn't any call for me to shout it:
        For he will do
        As he do do
            And there's no doing anything about it!

—from **The Rum Tum Tugger**
T. S. Eliot, English, 1888–1965

Curious Cats

In Art and Poetry

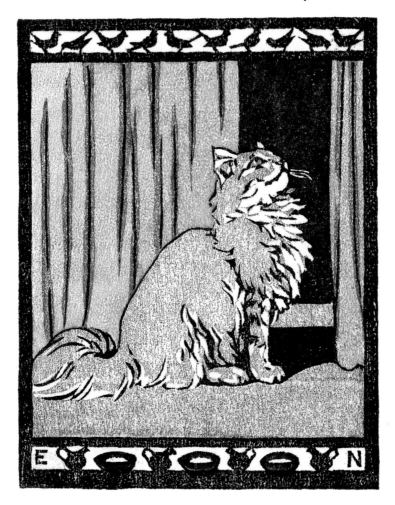

BRITISH MUSEUM 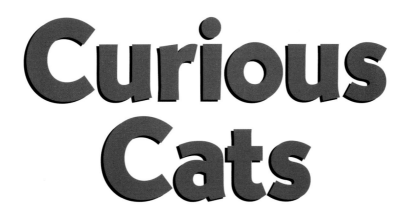 PRESS

in association with

THE METROPOLITAN MUSEUM OF ART

Except where noted, the works of art depicted in this book are from the collections of The Metropolitan Museum of Art.

COVER: *Cat* (detail), Toko (Oide Makoto), Japanese, 1841–1905, Ink and colors on silk, 14¾ x 11 in.

ENDPAPERS: *The Harrowing Tale of a Cat and a Guinea Pig, A Terrible End to a Goldfish, More Bread Than Butter!, The Cat and the Frog*, Théophile-Alexandre Steinlen, French, 1865–1923, Photorelief etchings from *Des Chats: Images Sans Paroles* (*Cats: Pictures Without Words*), 1898

TITLE PAGE: *Little Grey Cat*, Elizabeth Norton, American, 1887–?, Printed color woodcut, 5⅛ x 4⅜ in.

COPYRIGHT PAGE: *Two Cats*, Félix Vallotton, French, 1865–1925, Woodcut from *Pan*, 2½ x 2½ in., 1895

CONTENTS PAGE: Zoetrope strip, British, late 1860s

BACK FLAP: *A Terrible End to a Goldfish* (detail), Théophile-Alexandre Steinlen, French, 1865–1923, Photorelief etching from *Des Chats: Images Sans Paroles* (*Cats: Pictures Without Words*), 1898

BACK COVER: Poster calendar cover, Edward Penfield, American, 1866–1925, Commercial lithograph poster, 14 x 10⅛ in., 1897

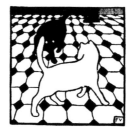

Published in Great Britain by
British Museum Press
A division of The British Museum Company Ltd
46 Bloomsbury Street
London WC1B 3QQ

First published 1999

For acknowledgments of the use of copyrighted material, please see page 48.

British Library Cataloguing-in-Publication Data
A catalogue record for this book is available from the British Library.

ISBN 0-7141-2729-9

Printed in Hong Kong

Produced by the Department of Special Publications,
The Metropolitan Museum of Art
All photography by The Metropolitan Museum of Art Photograph Studio,
except for pages 22–23, courtesy of the British Museum
Edited by William Lach; Designed by Anna Raff

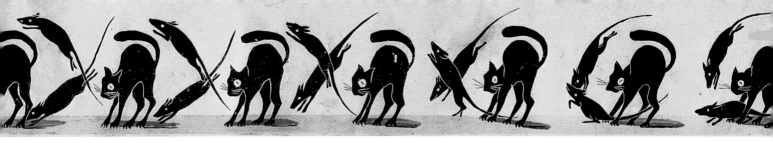

CONTENTS

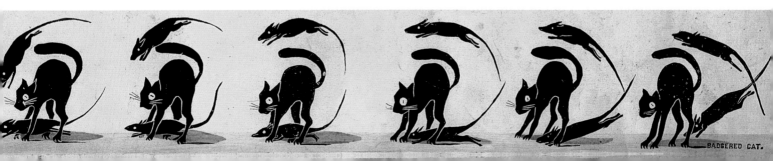

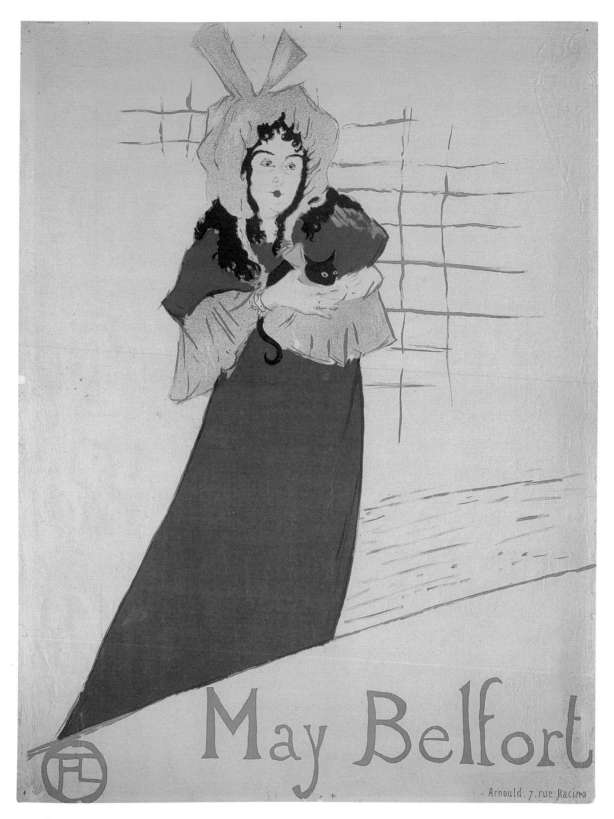

May Belfort
Henri de Toulouse-Lautrec, French, 1864–1901
Color lithograph, 31¼ x 21¼ in., 1895

INTRODUCTION

From nearly every continent, across epochs and dynasties, from the famous and the unknown, the works of art and poetry in this collection have one thing in common: the curious cat. In haiku, limerick, and nursery rhyme; in painting, sculpture, and zoetrope strip; the many feisty felines presented here share surprising similarities.

Christopher Smart's blessing to his pet Jeoffry, written in eighteenth-century England, describes the same tigerlike qualities visible in an Egyptian tomb painting made thirty centuries earlier. Emily Dickinson's suspenseful rhyme of a kitty and one lucky bird matches Francisco de Goya's court painting of the same spellbinding scenario. And, with soft fur, sharp whiskers, and golden eyes, the luxurious cat described in Jang'hi Yi's poem seems to stare out at us from the Indian watercolor next to it.

Whether fanciful, as in the Mother Goose rhyme of a pussycat that visited the queen, or ferocious, as in French primitivist Henri Rousseau's stirring *Repast of the Lion*, the felines in this collection do as they like, when they like. And just as cats are forever curious about the world, the art and poetry in this collection prove that the world was, is, and always will be deeply curious about cats.

—William Lach, Editor

Detail of a wood engraving
Gustave Doré, French, 1832–1883
From *Les Contes de Perrault* by Charles Perrault, Paris, 1899

The Tyger.

Tyger Tyger, burning bright,
In the forests of the night;
What immortal hand or eye,
Could frame thy fearful symmetry?

In what distant deeps or skies,
Burnt the fire of thine eyes?
On what wings dare he aspire?
What the hand, dare sieze the fire?

And what shoulder, & what art,
Could twist the sinews of thy heart?
And when thy heart began to beat,
What dread hand? & what dread feet?

What the hammer? what the chain,
In what furnace was thy brain?
What the anvil? what dread grasp,
Dare its deadly terrors clasp!

When the stars threw down their spears
And water'd heaven with their tears:
Did he smile his work to see?
Did he who made the Lamb make thee?

Tyger Tyger burning bright,
In the forests of the night:
What immortal hand or eye,
Dare frame thy fearful symmetry?

The Tyger

Tyger! Tyger! burning bright
In the forests of the night,
What immortal hand or eye
Could frame thy fearful symmetry?

In what distant deeps or skies
Burnt the fire of thine eyes?
On what wings dare he aspire?
What the hand dare seize the fire?

And what shoulder, & what art,
Could twist the sinews of thy heart?
And when thy heart began to beat,
What dread hand? & what dread feet?

What the hammer, what the chain?
In what furnace was thy brain?
What the anvil, what dread grasp
Dare its deadly terrors clasp?

When the stars threw down their spears,
And water'd heaven with their tears,
Did he smile his work to see?
Did he who made the Lamb make thee?

Tyger! Tyger! burning bright
In the forests of the night,
What immortal hand or eye
Dare frame thy fearful symmetry?

—William Blake, English, 1757–1827

The Tyger
William Blake, English, 1757–1827
From *Songs of Innocence and Experience*, 1789
Relief etching printed in color, 4⅞ x 2⅞ in.

The Lazy Pussy

There lives a good-for-nothing cat,
　　So lazy it appears,
That chirping birds can safely come
　　And light upon her ears.

And rats and mice can venture out
　　To nibble at her toes,
Or climb around and pull her tail,
　　And boldly scratch her nose.

Fine servants brush her silken coat
　　And give her cream for tea;—
Yet she's a good-for-nothing cat,
　　As all the world may see.

—Palmer Cox, American, 1840–1924

Spring Play in a Tang Garden (detail)
Chinese, Qing dynasty, 1644–1912
Handscroll, color on silk, 14¾ in. x 8 ft. 8 in.

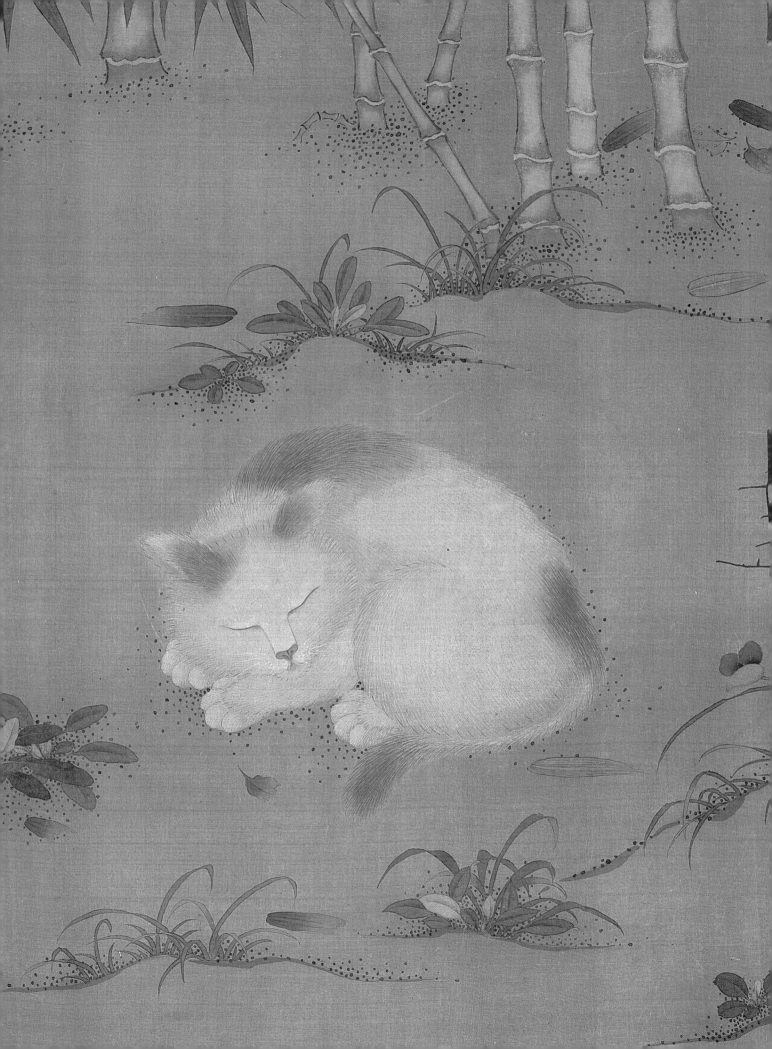

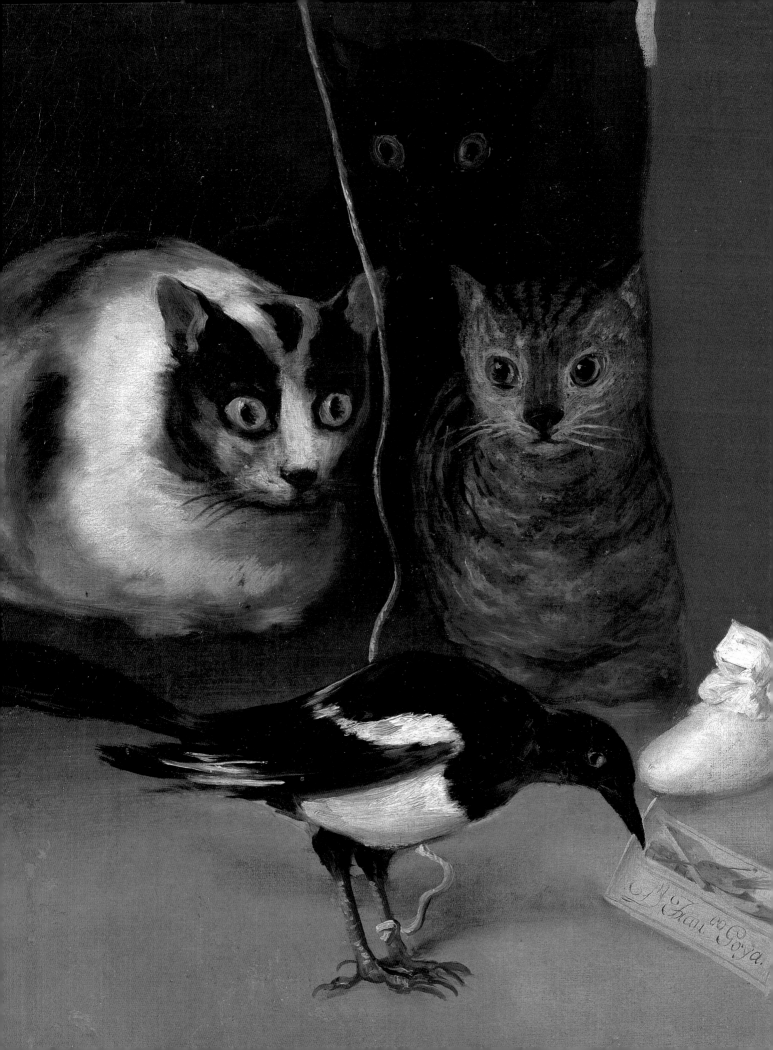

She Sights a Bird

She sights a Bird—she chuckles—
She flattens—then she crawls—
She runs without the look of feet—
Her eyes increase to Balls—

Her Jaws stir—twitching—hungry—
Her Teeth can hardly stand—
She leaps, but Robin leaped the first—
Ah, Pussy, of the Sand,

The Hopes so juicy ripening—
You almost bathed your Tongue—
When Bliss disclosed a hundred Toes—
And fled with every one—

—Emily Dickinson, American, 1830–1886

Don Manuel Osorio Manrique de Zuñiga (detail)
Francisco de Goya y Lucientes, Spanish, 1746–1828
Oil on canvas, 50 x 40 in.

The Three Little Kittens

Three little kittens lost their mittens;
   And they began to cry,
      "Oh, mother dear,
      We very much fear
That we have lost our mittens."
      "Lost your mittens!
      You naughty kittens!
Then you shall have no pie!"
      "Mee-ow, mee-ow, mee-ow."
"No, you shall have no pie."
      "Mee-ow, mee-ow, mee-ow."

The three little kittens found their mittens;
   And they began to cry,
      "Oh, mother dear,
      See here, see here!
See, we have found our mittens!"
      "Put on your mittens,
      You silly kittens,
And you may have some pie."
      "Purr-r, purr-r, purr-r,
Oh, let us have the pie!
      Purr-r, purr-r, purr-r."

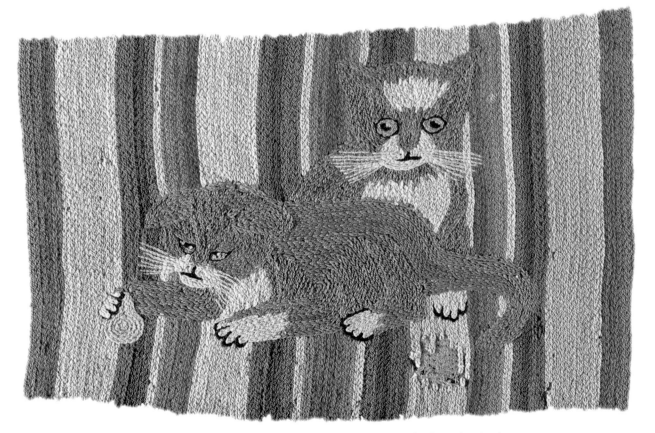

Details of an embroidered carpet
Zeruah Higley Guernsey Caswell, American, 1805–?1895
Wool embroidery on wool, 13 ft. 4 in. x 12 ft. 3 in., 1835

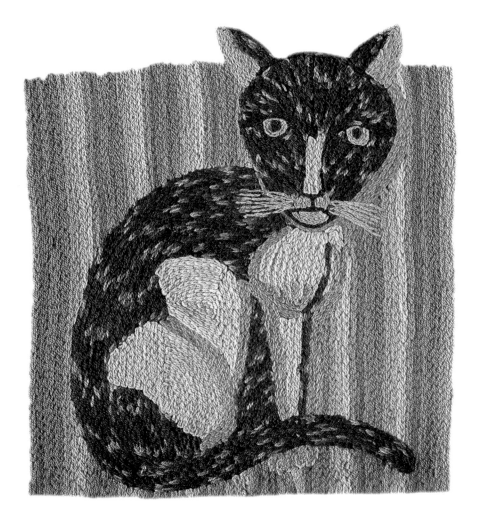

The three little kittens put on their mittens,
　　And soon ate up the pie;
　　　　"Oh, mother dear,
　　　　We greatly fear
That we have soiled our mittens!"
　　　　"Soiled your mittens!
　　　　You naughty kittens!"
Then they began to sigh,
　　"Mee-ow, mee-ow, mee-ow."
Then they began to sigh,
　　"Mee-ow, mee-ow, mee-ow."

The three little kittens washed their mittens,
　　And hung them out to dry;
　　　　"Oh, mother dear,
　　　　Do not you hear
That we have washed our mittens?"
　　　　"Washed your mittens!
　　　　Oh, you're good kittens!
But I smell a rat close by,
　　Hush, hush! Mee-ow, mee-ow."
"We smell a rat close by,
　　Mee-ow, mee-ow, mee-ow."

—Eliza Lee Follen, American, 1787–1860

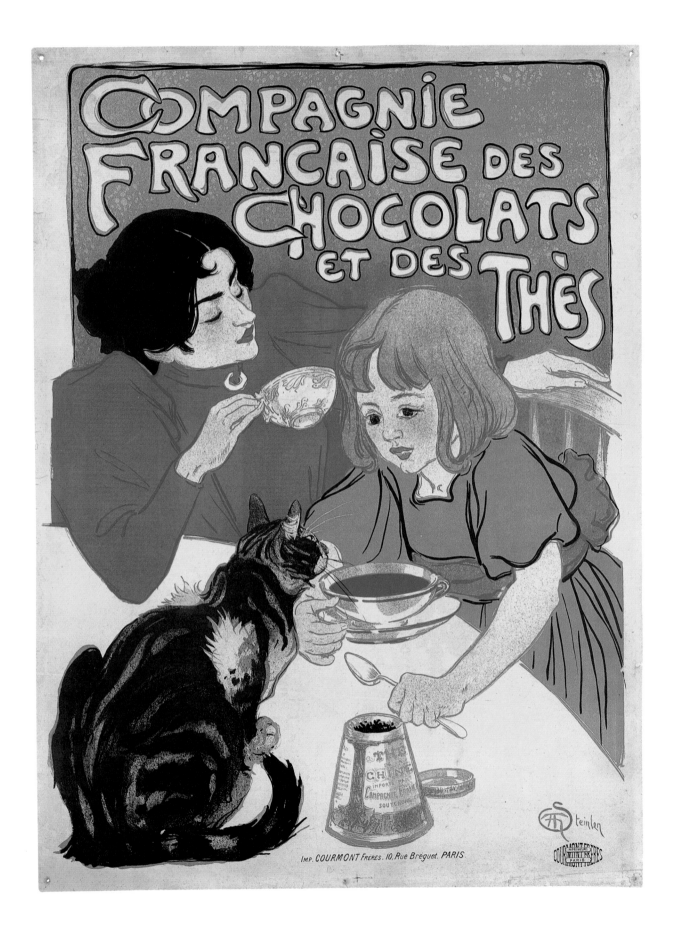

The Cats Have Come to Tea

What did she see—oh, what did she see,
As she stood leaning against the tree?
Why all the Cats had come to tea.

What a fine turn out—from round about,
All the houses had let them out,
And here they were with scamper and shout.

"Mew—mew—mew!" was all they could say,
And, "We hope we find you well to-day."

Oh, what should she do—oh, what should she do?
What a lot of milk they would get through;
For here they were with "Mew—mew—mew!"

She didn't know—oh, she didn't know,
If bread and butter they'd like or no;
They might want little mice, oh! oh! oh!

Dear me—oh, dear me,
All the cats had come to tea.

—Kate Greenaway, English, 1846–1901

Compagnie Française des Chocolats et des Thés
Théophile-Alexandre Steinlen, French, 1859–1923
Color lithograph poster, 40 x 30 in., 1899

A Lion

A lion in a zoo,
Shut up in a cage,
Lives a life
Of smothered rage.

A lion in the plain,
Roaming free,
Is happy as ever
A lion can be.

—Langston Hughes, American, 1902–1967

The Repast of the Lion (detail)
Henri-Julien-Félix Rousseau (le Douanier),
French, 1844–1910
Oil on canvas, 44¼ x 63 in.

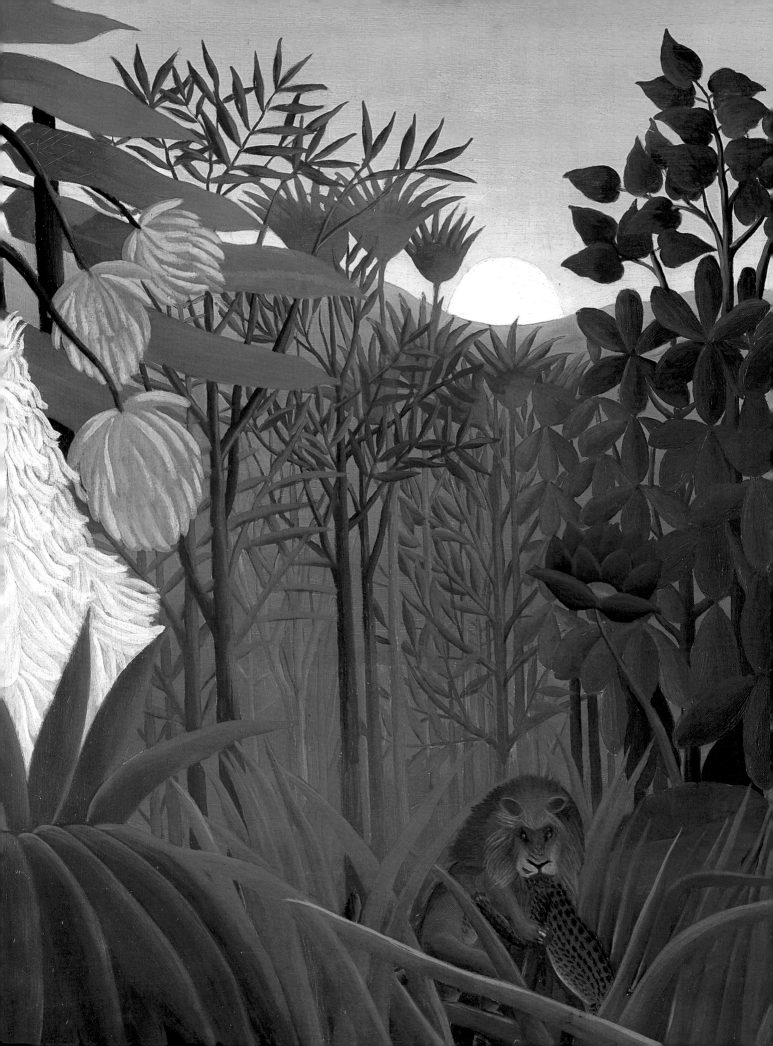

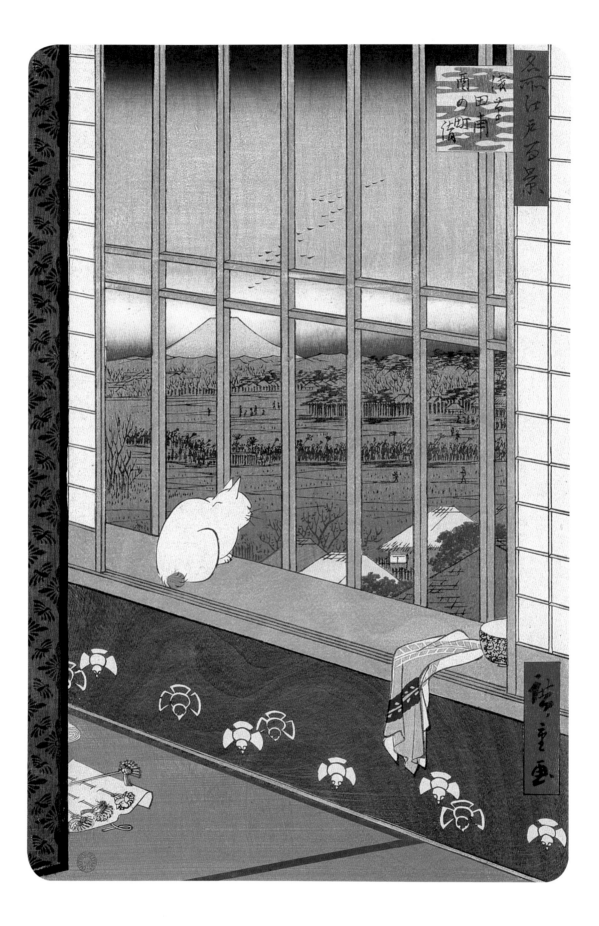

Three Cat Haiku

Flopped on the fan,
the big cat
 sleeping.

℔.

My cat,
frisking in the scale,
 records its weight.

℔.

The big cat
frisks its tail,
 toying with the butterfly.

—Kobayashi Issa, Japanese, 1763–1827
translation Robert Hass

Asakusa Rice Fields and Torinomachi Festival
Utagawa Hiroshige, Japanese, 1797–1858
From the series *One Hundred Famous Views of Edo*
Polychrome woodblock print, 13⅛ x 8⅞ in., 1857

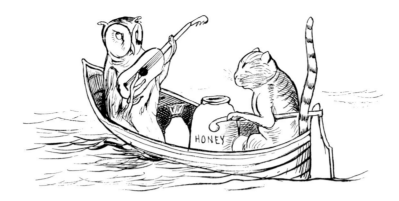

The Owl and the Pussy-cat

The Owl and the Pussy-cat went to sea
    In a beautiful pea-green boat,
They took some honey, and plenty of money,
    Wrapped up in a five-pound note.
The Owl looked up to the stars above,
    And sang to a small guitar,
"O lovely Pussy! O Pussy, my love,
    What a beautiful Pussy you are,
        You are,
        You are!
    What a beautiful Pussy you are!"

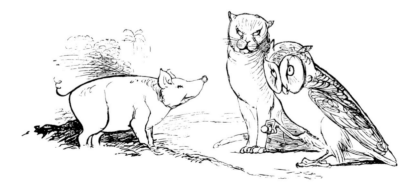

The Owl and the Pussy-cat
Edward Lear, English, 1812–1888
From *Nonsense Songs, Stories, Botany, and Alphabets*, 8⅞ in. x 6¼ in.
Published London, Robert John Bush, 1871
First edition, Quarto with wood engravings

Pussy said to the Owl, "You elegant fowl!
How charmingly sweet you sing!
O let us be married! too long we have tarried:
But what shall we do for a ring?"
They sailed away, for a year and a day,
To the land where the Bong-tree grows,
And there in a wood a Piggy-wig stood,
With a ring at the end of his nose,
His nose,
His nose,
With a ring at the end of his nose.

"Dear Pig, are you willing to sell for one shilling
Your ring?" Said the Piggy, "I will."
So they took it away, and were married next day
By the Turkey who lives on the hill.
They dined on mince, and slices of quince,
Which they ate with a runcible spoon;
And hand in hand, on the edge of the sand,
They danced by the light of the moon,
The moon,
The moon,
They danced by the light of the moon.

—Edward Lear, English, 1812–1888

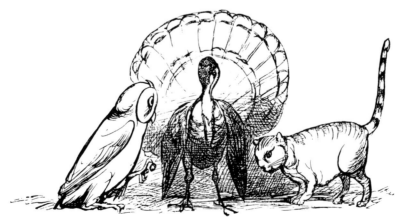

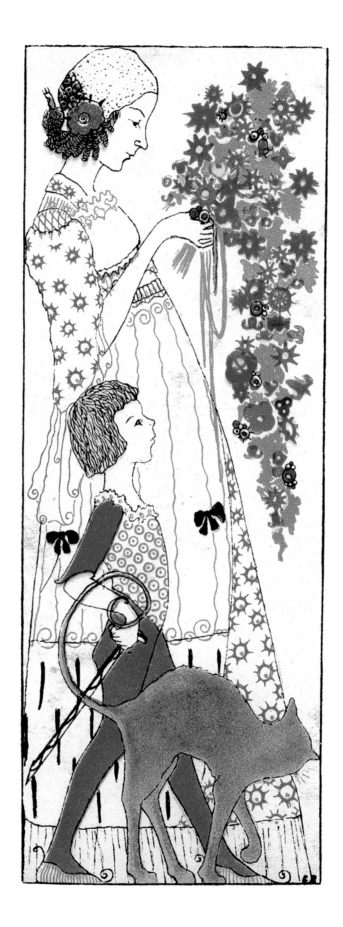

The Mysterious Cat

I saw a proud, mysterious cat,
I saw a proud, mysterious cat,
Too proud to catch a mouse or rat—
Mew, mew, mew.

But catnip she would eat, and purr,
But catnip she would eat, and purr.
And goldfish she did much prefer—
Mew, mew, mew.

I saw a cat—'twas but a dream,
I saw a cat—'twas but a dream
Who scorned the slave that brought her cream—
Mew, mew, mew.

Unless the slave were dressed in style,
Unless the slave were dressed in style,
And knelt before her all the while—
Mew, mew, mew.

Did you ever hear of a thing like that?
Did you ever hear of a thing like that?
Did you ever hear of a thing like that?
Oh, what a proud, mysterious cat.
Oh, what a proud, mysterious cat.
Oh, what a proud, mysterious cat.
Mew. . . mew. . . mew.

—Vachel Lindsay, American, 1879–1931

Woman, Child, and Cat
Detail of a color lithograph postcard
Unknown artist of the Wiener Werkstätte, Austrian, 5½ x 3½ in., ca. 1910

Three Cat Rhymes

Hey, diddle, diddle,
The cat and the fiddle,
The cow jumped over the moon;
The little dog laughed
To see such sport,
And the dish ran away with the spoon.

☙

Pussy-cat, pussy-cat, where have you been?
"I've been to London to look at the queen."
Pussy-cat, pussy-cat, what did you there?
"I frightened a little mouse under her chair."

☙

A cat came fiddling out of a barn,
With a pair of bagpipes under her arm;
She could sing nothing but fiddle-de-dee,
The mouse has married the bumble-bee;
Pipe, cat—dance, mouse—
We'll have a wedding at our good house.

—Mother Goose (Anonymous), English, 18th century

Hey! Diddle, Diddle, the Cat and the Fiddle!
Arthur Rackham, English, 1867–1939
From *Mother Goose, The Old Nursery Rhymes*, 9½ x 7¼ in.

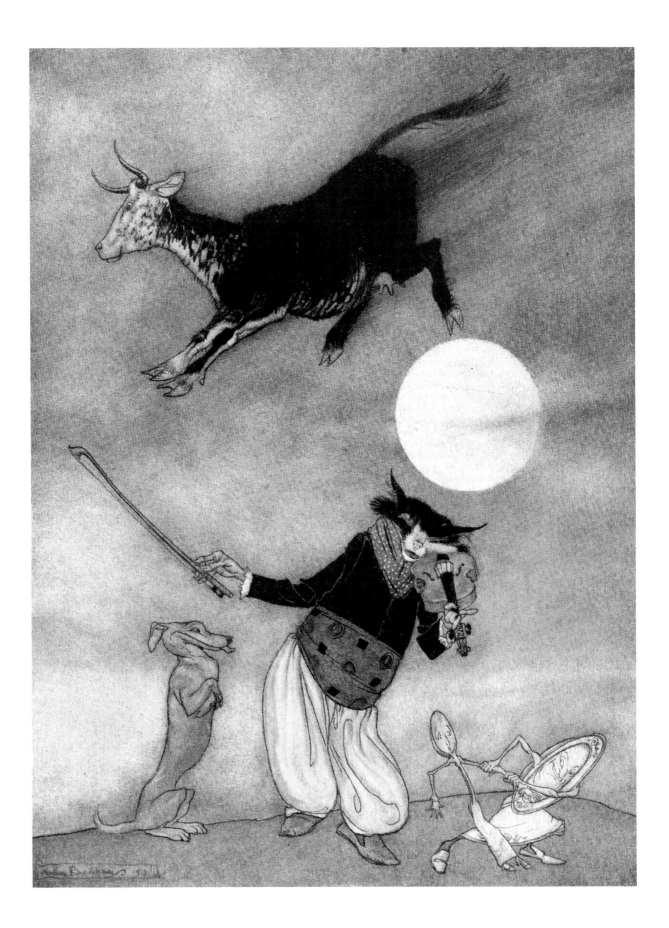

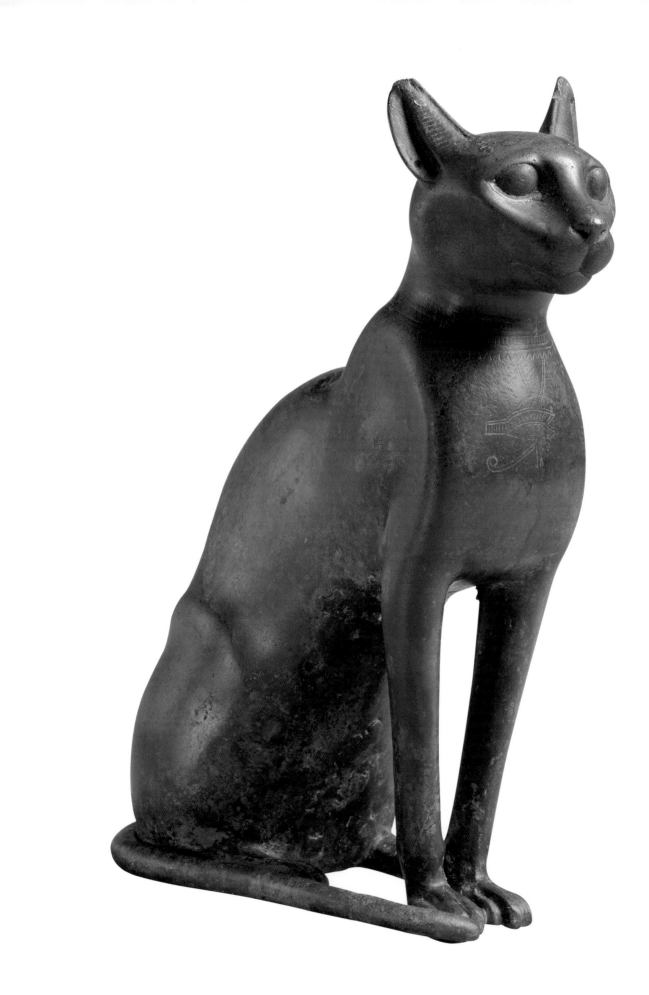

from Ode to the Cat

There was something wrong
with the animals:
their tails were too long, and they had
unfortunate heads.
Then they started coming together,
little by little
fitting together to make a landscape,
developing birthmarks, grace, pep.
But the cat,
only the cat
turned out finished,
and proud:
born in a state of total completion,
it sticks to itself and knows exactly what it wants.

Men would like to be fish or fowl,
snakes would rather have wings,
and dogs are would-be lions.
Engineers want to be poets,
flies emulate swallows,
and poets try hard to act like flies.
But the cat
wants nothing more than to be a cat,
and every cat is pure cat
from its whiskers to its tail,
from sixth sense to squirming rat,
from nighttime to its golden eyes.

—Pablo Neruda, Chilean, 1904–1973
translation Ken Krabbenhoft

Statue
Egyptian, Dynasty 26 or later (664–30 B.C.)
Bronze, H. 11 in.

from Dame Wiggins of Lee
and Her Seven Wonderful Cats

Dame Wiggins of Lee
    Was a worthy old soul
As e'er threaded a nee-
    dle or wash'd in a bowl:

She held mice and rats
    In such antipathee,
That seven fine cats
    Kept Dame Wiggins of Lee.

The rats and mice scared
    By this fierce-whiskered crew,
The poor seven cats
    Soon had nothing to do;

So, as anyone idle
    She ne'er loved to see,
She sent them to school,
    Did Dame Wiggins of Lee.

The master soon wrote
    That they all of them knew
How to read the word "milk"
    And to spell the word "mew,"

And they all washed their faces
    Before they took tea.
Were there ever such dears?
    Said Dame Wiggins of Lee.

—John Ruskin, English, 1819–1900

Woodcut
Kate Greenaway, English, 1846–1901
From *Dame Wiggins of Lee and Her Seven Wonderful Cats*, 7¼ x 4⁹⁄₁₆ in.

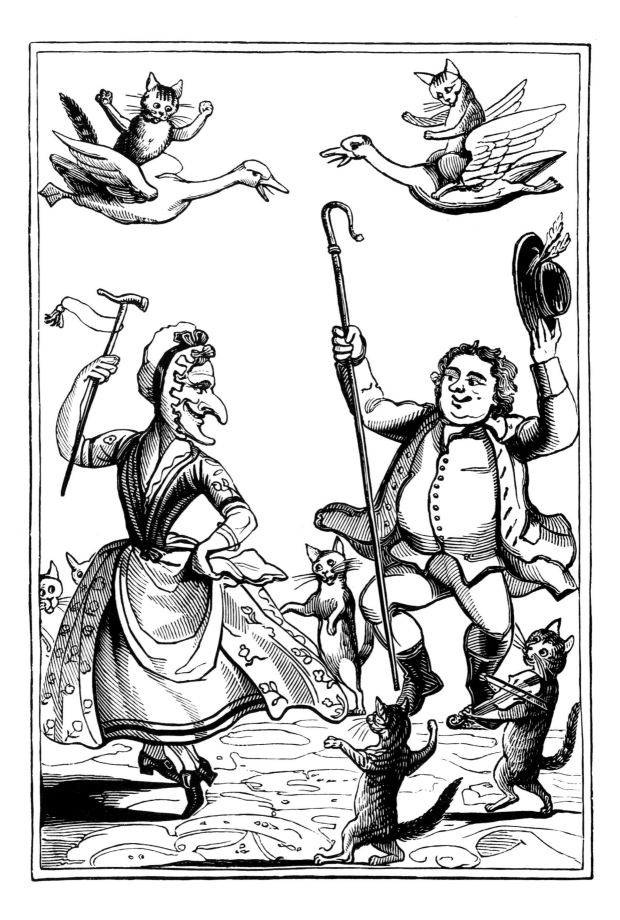

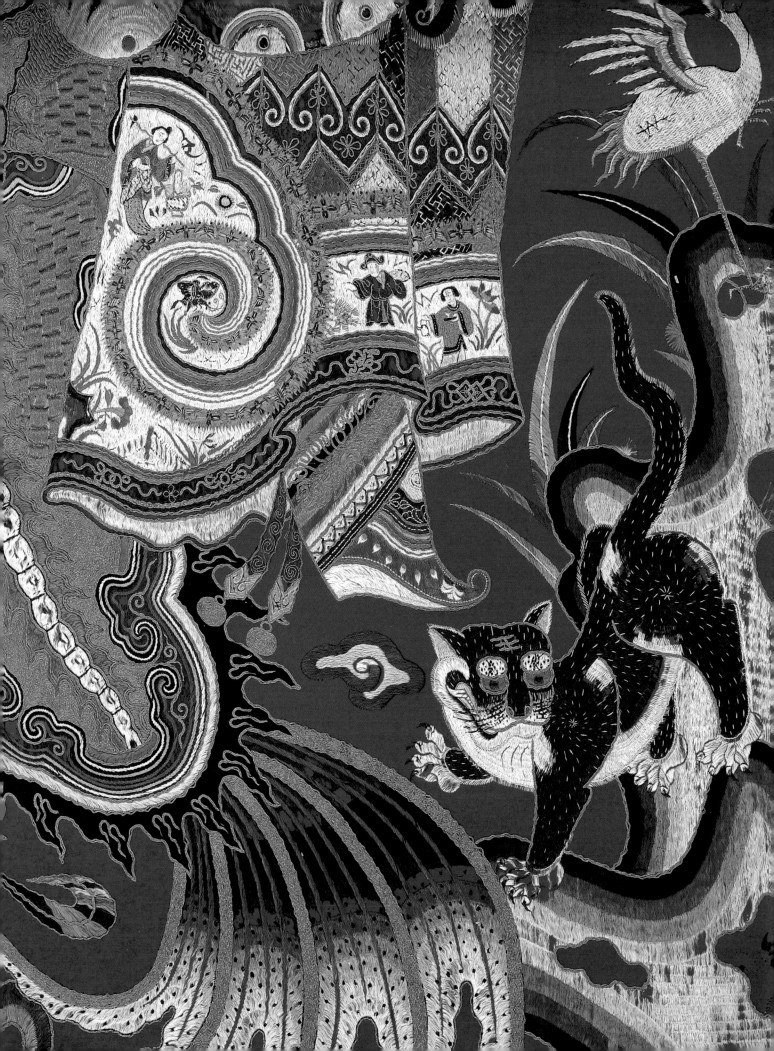

from **The Cat and the Cock**

Once a certain cat and cock,
Friendship founded on a rock,
Lived together in a house
In the land of Fledermaus.
Each loved music in his way,
And the cock, at break of day
Chanted: "Cock-a-doodle-doo!
Kiki-riki—Kuk-ru-koo!",
While his cat-friend, in the middle
Of the night, would play the fiddle.
Sometimes they would play together
—Handsome fur and fancy feather—
And the pair would dance and sing
While the house with joy would ring.

—Vikram Seth, Indian, b. 1952

Detail of an embroidered theater curtain
Chinese, 19th century
Wool flannel, silk, and metallic thread, 10 ft. 8¾ in. x 6 ft. 8 in.

Nipping Pussy's Feet in Fun

This is not kind.

Oh Mr. Pussy-Cat
My, you are sweet!
How do you get about so much
On those tiny feet?
Nip, nip; miaou, miaou,
Tiny little feet,
Nip, nip pussy-cat
My, you are sweet!

Cat Asks Mouse Out

But then neither is this.

Mrs. Mouse
Come out of your house
It is a fine sunny day
And I am waiting to play.

Bring the little mice too
And we can run to and fro.

—Stevie Smith, English, 1902–1971

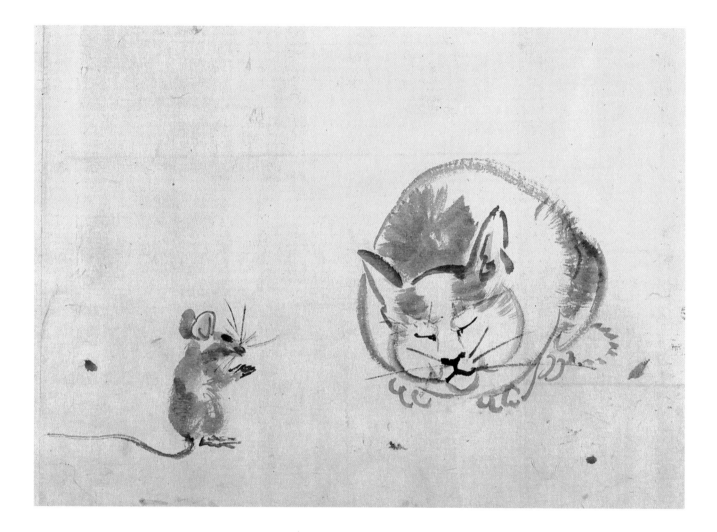

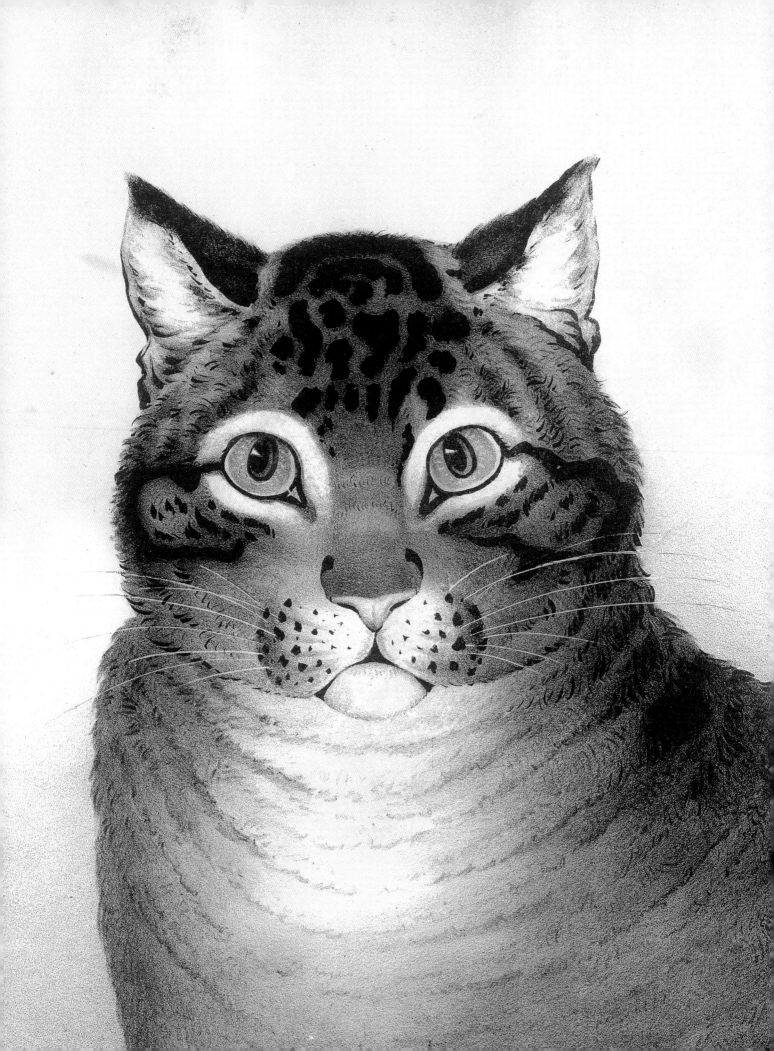

from **A Fable of the Widow and Her Cat**

A widow kept a favorite cat,
    At first a gentle creature;
But when he was grown sleek and fat,
With many a mouse, and many a rat,
    He soon disclosed his nature.

The fox and he were friends of old,
    Nor could they now be parted;
They nightly slunk to rob the fold,
Devoured the lambs, the fleeces sold,
    And Puss grew lion-hearted.

—Jonathan Swift, English, 1667–1745

The Favorite Cat (detail)
Nathaniel Currier, publisher, American, 1813–1888
Hand-colored lithograph, 12⅛ x 8¼ in., ca. 1840–60

Kilkenny Cats

There once were two cats of Kilkenny,
Each thought there was one cat too many;
So they fought and they fit,
And they scratched and they bit,
Till, excepting their nails
And the tips of their tails,
Instead of two cats there weren't any.

—Traditional

Harper's July (detail)
Edward Penfield, American, 1866–1925
Commercial lithograph poster, 14 x 20 in, 1898

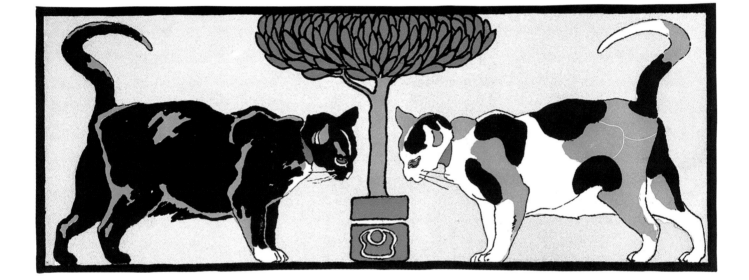

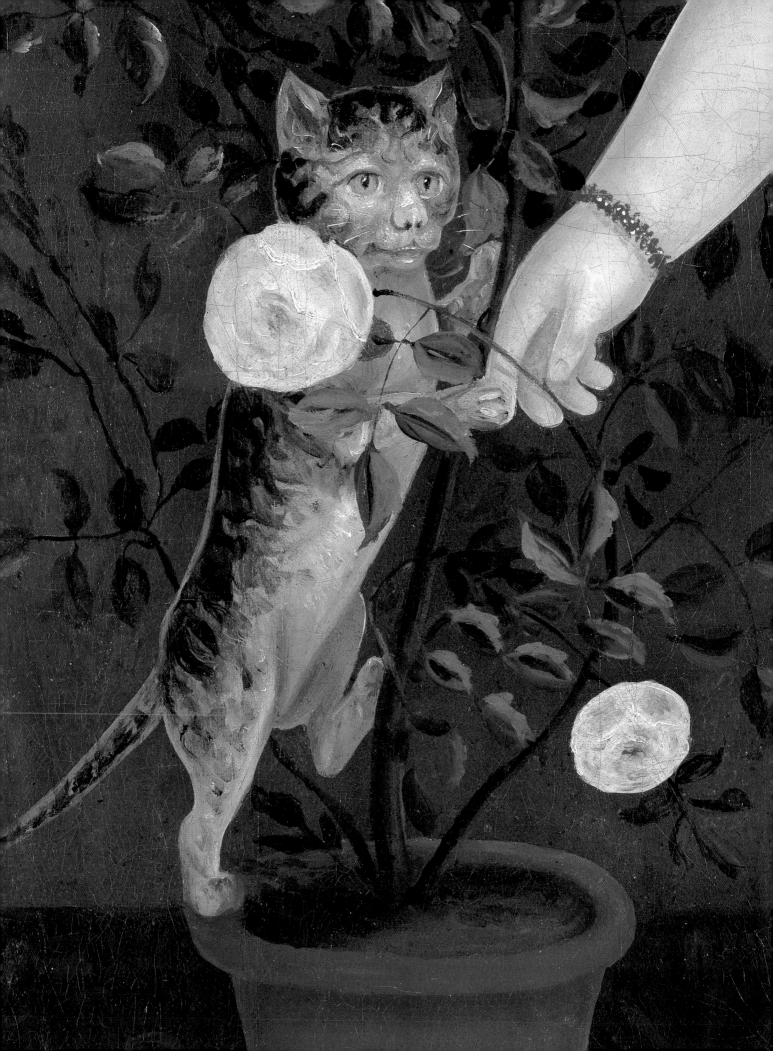

Poem

As the cat
climbed over
the top of

the jamcloset
first the right
forefoot

carefully
then the hind
stepped down

into the pit of
the empty
flowerpot

—William Carlos Williams, American, 1883–1963

Emma Homan (detail)
John Bradley, American, active 1832–47
Oil on canvas, 34 x 27⅛ in., ca. 1843–44

from **The Kitten and Falling Leaves**

See the Kitten on the wall,
Sporting with the leaves that fall,
Withered leaves—one—two—and three—
From the lofty elder-tree!
Through the calm and frosty air
Of this morning bright and fair,
Eddying round and round they sink
Softly, slowly: one might think,
From the motions that are made,
Every little leaf conveyed
Sylph or Faery hither tending,—
To this lower world descending,
Each invisible and mute,
In his wavering parachute.
—But the Kitten, how she starts,

Crouches, stretches, paws, and darts!
First at one, and then its fellow
Just as light and just as yellow;
There are many now—now one—
Now they stop and there are none:
What intenseness of desire
In her upward eye of fire!
With a tiger-leap half-way
Now she meets the coming prey,
Lets it go as fast, and then
Has it in her power again:
Now she works with three or four,
Like an Indian conjurer;
Quick as he in feats of art,
Far beyond in joy of heart.

—William Wordsworth, English, 1770–1850

Cat and Yellow Butterfly (detail)
Xu Beihong, Chinese, 1895–1953
Hanging scroll, ink and colors on paper, 44 x 21¼ in., 1941

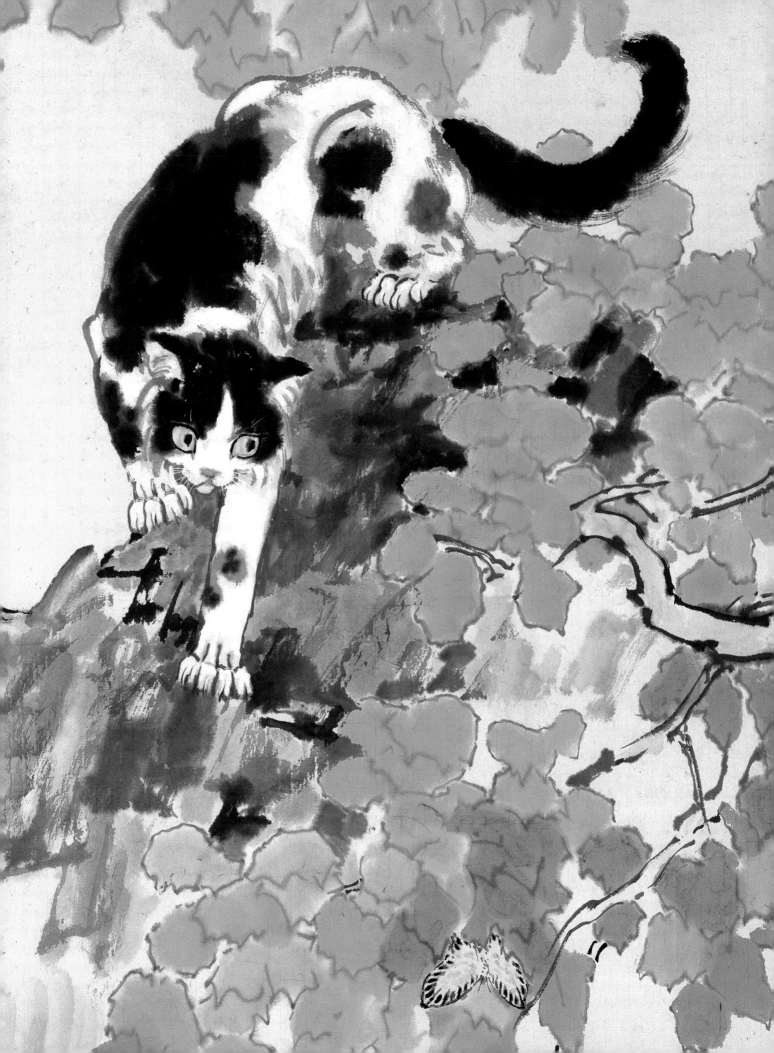

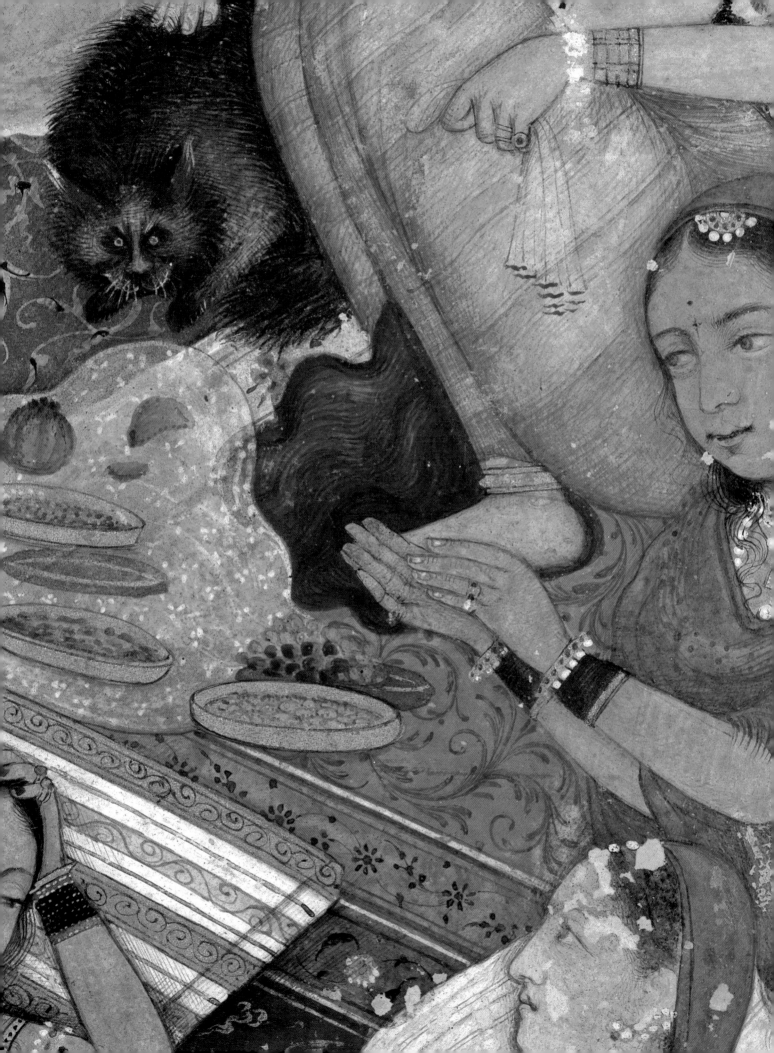

The Spring Is a Cat

On a cat's fur soft as pollen,
The mild Spring's fragrance lingers.

In a cat's eyes round as golden bells,
The mad Spring's flame glows.

On a cat's gently closed lips,
The soft Spring's drowsiness lies.

On a cat's sharp whiskers,
The green Spring's life dances.

—Jang'hi Yi, Korean, 1902–1928
translation Chang Soo Ko

Zenana Scene (detail)
Indian, 18th century
Opaque watercolor and gold on paper, 7⅞ x 5 in.

from Jubilate Agno

For I will consider my Cat Jeoffry.

For he is the servant of the Living God duly and daily serving him.

For at the first glance of the glory of God in the East he worships in his way.

For is this done by wreathing his body seven times round with elegant quickness.

For then he leaps up to catch the musk, which is the blessing of God upon his prayer.

For he rolls upon prank to work it in.

For having done duty and received blessing he begins to consider himself.

For this he performs in ten degrees.

For first he looks upon his fore-paws to see if they are clean.

For secondly he kicks up behind to clear away there.

For thirdly he works it upon stretch with the fore-paws extended.

For fourthly he sharpens his paws by wood.

For fifthly he washes himself.

For Sixthly he rolls upon wash.

For Seventhly he fleas himself, that he may not be interrupted upon the beat.

For Eighthly he rubs himself against a post.

For Ninthly he looks up for his instructions.

For Tenthly he goes in quest of food.

For having consider'd God and himself he will consider his neighbor.

For if he meets another cat he will kiss her in kindness.

For when he takes his prey he plays with it to give it chance.

For one mouse in seven escapes by his dallying.

For when his day's work is done his business more properly begins.

For he keeps the Lord's watch in the night against the adversary.

For he counteracts the powers of darkness by his electrical skin and glaring eyes.

For he counteracts the Devil, who is death, by brisking about the life.

For in his morning orisons he loves the sun and the sun loves him.

For he is of the tribe of Tiger.

—Christopher Smart, English, 1722–1771

Detail of a facsimile of a wall painting in the Tomb of Sennedjem
Egyptian (Thebes), ca. 1275 B.C.

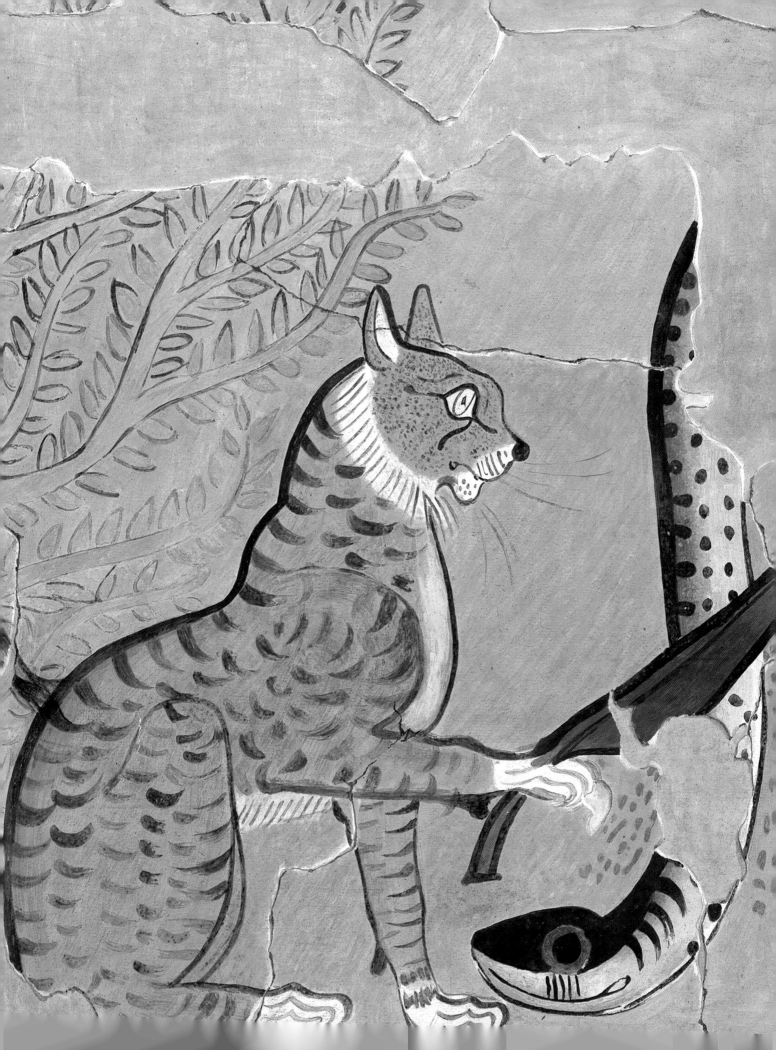

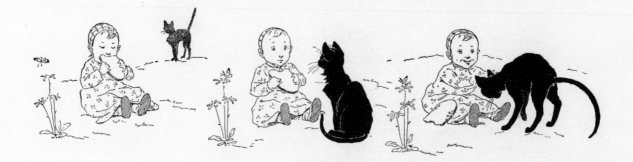

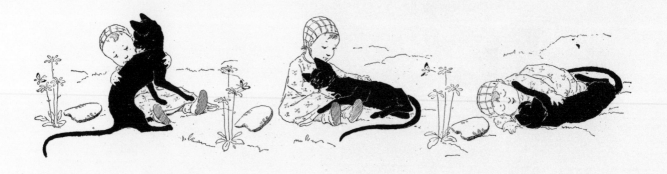

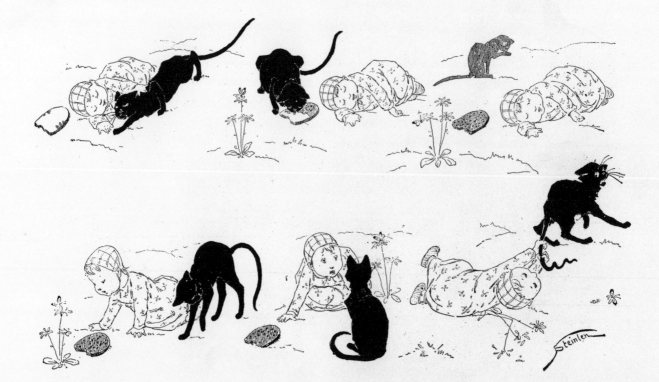